The Rainbow Spirit in Creation

The Rainbow Spirit in Creation

A Reading of Genesis 1

Jasmine Corowa

Artist

Norman Habel

Translator and Editor

for

The Rainbow Spirit Elders

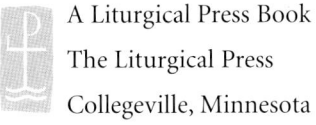

A Liturgical Press Book
The Liturgical Press
Collegeville, Minnesota

Cover and book design by Ann Blattner.

1	2	3	4	5	6	7	8

Library of Congress Cataloging-in-Publication Data

Corowa, Jasmine.
  The Rainbow Spirit in creation : a reading of Genesis 1 / Jasmine Corowa, artist ; Norman Habel, translator for the Rainbow Spirit Elders.
      p.   cm.
  Text translated from Aborigine ms., never before published.
  ISBN 0-8146-2716-1 (alk. paper)
  1. Corowa, Jasmine—Catalogs.   2. Bible. O.T. Genesis I—Illustrations—Catalogs.   3. Australian aborigines—Religion.   I. Habel, Norman C.
II. Rainbow Spirit Elders.   III. Title.

N7405.C665   2000
759.994—dc21   00-030164

THE WORKS OF ART in this set of paintings seek to capture the force of the creation story in Genesis 1 through the eyes of the Rainbow Spirit Elders from Queensland in Australia. In particular, they are the work of the artist Jasmine Corowa, a daughter of one of these elders. These indigenous elders explore how their Christian faith can be expressed in terms of their Aboriginal culture and spirituality. A more detailed expression of their thinking is found in the book *Rainbow Spirit Theology,* published by HarperCollins Religious (Blackburn, Australia, 1997). The translator and editor is Norman Habel, who worked with the elders to facilitate publication of this theology.

In the Beginning

*I*n the beginning,
when God created the sky and the land,
the land was unformed and empty;
darkness was upon the face of the deep,
and the Spirit of God glided over the face
of the waters.

Light

And God said, "Let there be light!"

And there was light.

God saw the light was good.

And God split the darkness with the light.

God called the light *Day*

and the darkness *Night*.

It was evening and morning.

DAY ONE.

The Sky

And God said, "Let there be a canopy
in the midst of the waters,
and let it split the waters."
So God made the canopy
and split the waters that were under the canopy
from the waters that were above the canopy.
And it was so.
God called the canopy *Sky*.
It was evening and morning.

DAY TWO.

The Land

And God said, "Let the waters under the sky
be gathered together in one place,
and let dry ground be revealed."
And it was so.
God called the dry ground *Land*.
And the waters that were gathered together
God called *Seas*.
And God saw it was good.

The Bush

*T*hen God said, "Let the land bring forth vegetation:
plants that produce seeds,
every species of fruit tree that bears fruit with
a seed in it upon the land."
And it was so.
The land brought forth vegetation:
every kind of plant that produces seeds,
and every species of tree that produces fruit with
a seed in it.
And God saw that it was good.
It was morning and evening.

DAY THREE.

The Sun and Moon

And God said, "Let there be lights in the canopy
of the sky
to split the day and the night.
And let them be for signs and seasons,
days and years.
And let there be lights in the canopy of the sky
to provide light on the land."
And it was so.
God made the two great lights,
the greater light to rule the day,
the lesser light to rule the night
and the stars.
And God saw that it was good.
It was morning and evening.

DAY FOUR.

Birds and Sea Life

*A*nd God said, "Let the waters bring forth swarms

of living things,

and let birds fly over the land across the canopy

of the sky."

God also created great sea monsters

and every species of living thing that swarms

in the waters

and every species of winged bird.

And God saw that it was good.

God sang them and said,

"Be fruitful and multiply and fill the waters in the seas,

and let the birds multiply on the land."

It was evening and morning.

DAY FIVE.

The Animals

And God said, "Let the land bring forth every
species of living creature:
cattle and creeping things and wild life on the land."
And it was so.
God made every species of wild life on the land,
and every species of cattle,
and every creeping thing on the ground.
And God saw that it was good.

Human Beings

*T*hen God said, "Let us make ground beings
in our image,
after our likeness;
and let them rule over the fish of the sea,
the birds of the air, the cattle,
the wild life on the land,
and every creeping thing on the land."
And God saw that it was good.
So God created ground beings in God's image,
male and female God created them.
God sang them, and said,
"Be fruitful and multiply
and fill the land and subdue it.
Rule over the fish of the sea, the birds of the air
and every living thing that creeps on the ground."

Rest

So the sky, the land, and all their company
were completed.
On the seventh day God completed the work
to be done,
and rested on the seventh day from the work
that was done.
God sang the seventh day and made it sacred,
because on it God rested from all the work
of creation to be done.
This is the family story about when sky and land
were created.

A Rainbow Spirit Reading
of
Genesis 1

Deep, dark colors are used to portray the unformed land existing below the deep primal waters. As the Rainbow Spirit has not yet formed light or created anything, one color was chosen for the background—a dark gray, that conveys a sense of nothingness and mystery. Pithalo blue, pithalo green, and a darker gray are chosen as the colors of the ocean. The land consists of the traditional earth colors —ochre reds and oranges that capture the different sands of Australia. As the Rainbow Snake is still lying within the earth—and waiting—black and white adds to the mystery of the Creator Spirit still entombed. At the same time the image of the Rainbow Spirit can be discerned gliding across the waters—almost camouflaged. To enhance the feeling of an unformed land, the different colored dots are not joined together. The latent shapes and designs in the Rainbow Spirit eventually appear in life and creation.

*H*ere the Rainbow Spirit is still entombed—waiting, ready. From the Spirit erupt flashes of lightning—light! Where the lightning emerges from the Spirit, the lightning remains the same base color. The lightning/light emerges from the dark entombed mystery at the center. The lightning/light that escapes from the earth is alive, bright, functional. It splits the dark waters. The lightning/light (off white) also represents day; the darkness of the waters (gray) represents night. This subtle division of day and night does not reach its full potential until sun, moon, and stars are created on Day Four.

*T*he Rainbow Spirit remains deep within the unformed land surrounded by the deep waters. A great canopy is formed in the midst of the waters to split the waters. God calls the canopy "sky." The white outline, like the lightning of Day Two, highlights how the canopy splits the waters. The colors chosen represent evening and morning, colors seen in the sky at these times of day.

*T*his scene is pivotal to the sequence of creation scenes that follow. The land that was hidden beneath the waters is "revealed" from below. The waters that once surrounded the land are now gathered to one place and called "seas." These waters that were once gray are now blue. The forming of the land is highlighted by the dots now being joined together. The "land" that was once dark gray is now alive and green. The outline of the earth/tomb surrounding the land is now broken open and the Rainbow Spirit is released/revealed. The Spirit is now awake in the land so it sheds its black and white skin and displays its living colors. These colors represent the colors used in the other creation scenes. The sky too is now more vibrant because of the power and sparkling colors of the Spirit. Everything is bright and new.

*T*he Rainbow Spirit creates the bush, vibrant with green life. The colors reflect the hues of rainforest, desert plants, scrub. The light green strokes through dark green areas represent tree roots. All the other colors—white, yellow, and black—represent nutrients, rocks, decaying wood that provide food for trees. The yellow and green objects filled with white dots are the seeds from which plant life emerges.

*T*he Rainbow Spirit rises up from the land to split the sky into day and night. This splitting is expressed by the white line. This action also locates the parts of creation in their place. Warm colors identify the sun. The colors coming from the sun represent heat—the brightest red is next to the sun but softens as the color moves away from the sun. The yellow represents the sun's rays. The sky is pitch black at night in the bush far away from lights of the city. Stars and moon are stark white against the black night.

*T*he birds are blue to represent the sky where they belong. The brightness of the sun lights up the whole sky. The Rainbow Spirit assumes the shape of the waves to indicate that the Rainbow Spirit is linked to the land/sea and continues to reside within the creation. The sea life below is vibrant with living creatures and plant life. The term "sing" is used here and later to capture the meaning of the Hebrew word usually translated "bless." In many Aboriginal cultures to "sing" with a ritual is to empower with life, which is the essence of the ancient rite of blessing.

$\mathcal{T}$he land, potent with life, brings forth every species of animal. Each animal is emerging from different levels in the land as the Rainbow Spirit watches—filled with delight. A crocodile encompasses a water hole, a goanna* crawls up a tree, butterflies brush the sky, and an emu inhabits the drier parts of the earth—parts highlighted by the different undercolors of the land, some green and some orange. The kangaroo leaps between these areas.

goanna—a large lizard of the family Varanidae

$\mathcal{T}$he world is clearly divided into earth, sea, land, and sky, the domains where humans travel. They are different sizes and genders, representing different ages—both male and female. Each is also a different color, representing the skin colors and ground colors around the world—colors in the image of the Rainbow Spirit. Humans are "ground beings," that is, beings who come from the ground. The Hebrew word for human being or Adam (ʾadam) is derived from the word for ground (ʾadamah). Human beings, land, and the creatures of the land are kin in the text and in most Aboriginal Australian cultures.

*A*ll of creation is completed and a day of rest is announced. The Rainbow Spirit is now the central focus of all creation. This image, like a logo design, is intended to express togetherness in a world where each part is created to complement the other. The day of rest is also the day of celebration. Around the Rainbow Spirit, human beings are celebrating with a corroboree.* All of life—each in its own habitat—is also celebrating. In the circles around the dance ground appear land animals, sea animals, and those that dwell between. The sky surrounds the land and the sun surrounds the sky. Above the sun is the rainbow, the gift of the Rainbow Spirit to the land and all that dwells within it. The colors in the rainbow are displayed above for all to see and marvel—for they are the colors of creation already captured on the land below and the very colors of the Creator Spirit at the center.

corroboree—an assembly of Aborigines typified by singing and dancing, sometimes associated with traditional sacred rites